Kid Pix:®
Simple Projects

Primary

Editorial Project Manager
Charles Payne, M.A., M.F.A

Editor-in-Chief
Sharon Coan, M.S. Ed.

Art Director
Elayne Roberts

Art Coordination Assistant
Cheri Macoubrie Wilson

Imaging
James Edward Grace

Production Manager
Phil Garcia

Acknowledgements
Kid Pix® is a registered trademark of Brøderbund Software, Inc.

Publishers
Rachelle Cracchiolo, M.S. Ed.
Mary Dupuy Smith, M.S. Ed.

Authors

Marsha Lifter, M.A.,
and Marian E. Adams

Teacher Created Materials, Inc.
6421 Industry Way
Westminster, CA 92683
www.teachercreated.com

©1999 Teacher Created Materials, Inc.
Reprinted, 2000, b
Made in U.S.A.
ISBN-1-57690-412-4

The classroom teacher may reproduce copies of materials in this book for classroom use only. The reproduction of any part for an entire school or school system is strictly prohibited. No part of this publication may be transmitted, stored, or recorded in any form without written permission from the publisher.

Table of Contents

Introduction to Kid Pix: Simple Projects 4

Simple Projects

Mother's Day Certificate 5

Make a Shape Book 9

Make A Postcard 15

A Teepee 19

My Own Flash Cards 22

Alphabet Code 25

An Action Picture 29

Make a Puzzle 32

City—Country? 36

Put All the Eggs in the Basket 40

Elephant Valentines 43

My Own Game Board 49

Puppet People 54

Fun Writing 57

Pinwheels 61

Two Kids—One Computer 64

Hidden Letters 65

Remember? 66

Where Did It Go? 67

Erase a Shape 68

What's Wrong with This Picture 69

Tell Me What to Draw 70

Table of Contents *(cont.)*

Copy My Picture 71

Connect the Shapes 72

Where's My Tail? 73

Follow Me 74

Picture It! 75

Make Something from Nothing 76

Dot-to-Dot Picture 77

Yum Yum—Ice-Cream Sundaes 78

Tic Tac Toe 79

Hangman for Two 80

Roll It 81

Tips and Tricks with Kid Pix 82

Kid Pix Projects Templates 84

The CD-ROM 96

Introduction to Kid Pix: Simple Projects

Upon the success *of Kid Pix* for *Terrified Teachers K–2* and *Kid Pix for Terrified Teachers 3–5*, teachers have been asking for more activities for their students.

Here are the newest activities for students using *Kid Pix*. In addition to new activities which students can do following easy step-by-step directions, there are activities for two students using one computer and *Kid Pix* to do together.

A new feature of *Kid Pix: Simple Projects* is a CD-ROM containing all the examples from the book and a series of templates which students can use. Students use these interactive templates to create their own unique publications. They follow the directions, add artwork and words, and then save the file with their initials and print. The templates were designed to encourage using thinking and computer skills as well as creative thought.

The empowering of students to create something unique using a computer is overwhelming when you think about it. Imagine all the power of computing at the fingers of students. *Kid Pix* enables children to enter a world of technology at their level of understanding.

Enjoy using *Kid Pix: Simple Projects K–2* and *Kid Pix for Terrified Teachers K–2* with your students.

Using *Kid Pix*

Classroom teachers who work with younger children will find many uses for the activities in this book. Many of the projects can be adapted for use in other grades and in special programs. English language development, special education, and gifted and talented students will find delight in their *Kid Pix* discoveries.

Duplicate the project directions, mount them on cardstock, laminate them, and place them next to the computer. You might want to duplicate and mount the examples also so students have an idea of how the project might look. The examples are merely a jumping-off point for students because their projects will be much more creative.

The projects are written at a primary level and encompass the different disciplines found in the primary grades. As students work on the projects, they will also be honing their computer skills. As you become more familiar with *Kid Pix*, you will find myriad ways in which to use it in your classroom.

#2412 Kid Pix: Simple Projects — 4 — *© Teacher Created Materials, Inc.*

Simple Projects

Mother's Day Certificate

This Project

A certificate for your mother for Mother's Day is a really good present to give. First of all, it is from you and tells your mother that you know about all the nice things that she does for you.

1. Think about all the many things that you mother does for you. She makes your meals, helps you with homework, takes you to places you need to go, and, most of all, she loves you. What would you like to tell her on this special day?
2. First, make the frame for the certificate and then write the message.
3. There are several choices from which to choose for frames.

- Select the Rubber Stamps tool and find a stamp that would look good as a frame. It might be a bow, maybe the sun, or anything that would look good repeated. Click on the rubber stamp and stamp it all around the edges of the screen to make a frame.

- Select the Wacky Brush tool and choose one of the options that would make a good frame. The bubbles might be good or maybe the hands, bows, or hearts from the options menu.

- Another frame choice might be to make straight lines with the Straight Line tool in different colors and put rubber stamps in each corner.

4. Type in what you want to say to your mother.

5. Use the Typewriter tool or select Goodies and choose Type Text. Choose a color from the color palette before you start typing in your message. You could even have many different colors in your message.
6. Print your certificate for your mother. Select Print from the File menu.

What Else Can I Do?

1. Make certificates for friends and other relatives.
2. You can make certificates for winners of games and for awards from clubs.

© Teacher Created Materials, Inc. #2412 Kid Pix: Simple Projects

Simple Projects

Mother's Day Certificate *(cont.)*

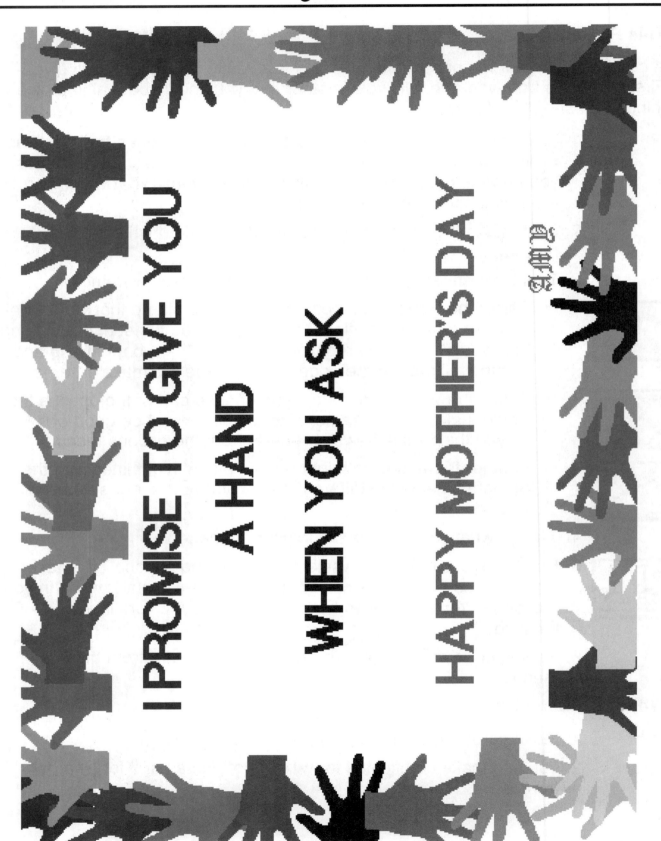

Mother's Day Certificate (cont.)

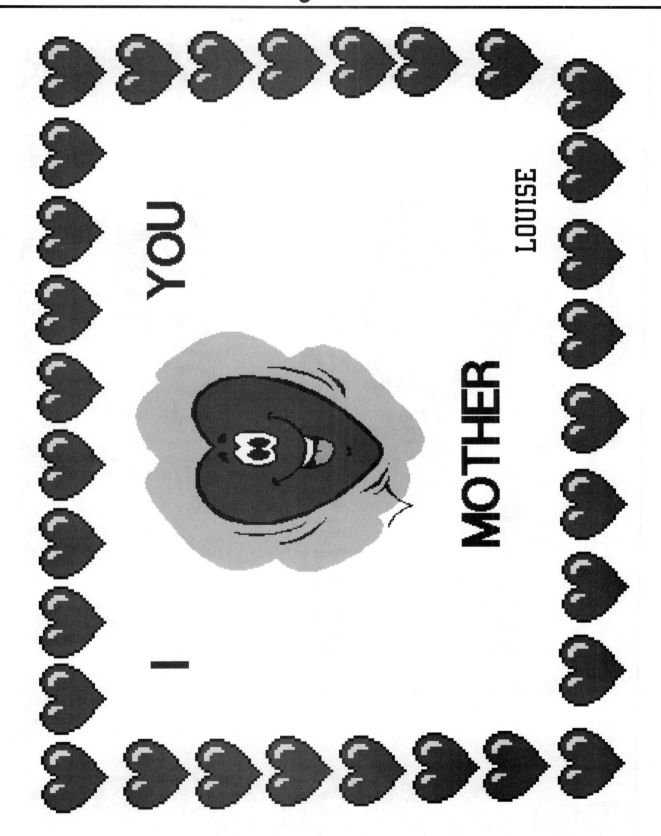

I YOU MOTHER LOUISE

Simple Projects

Mother's Day Certificate (cont.)

#2412 Kid Pix: Simple Projects © Teacher Created Materials, Inc.

Simple Projects

Make a Shape Book

This Project

You are going to create a shape on the screen that will be the cover for a book that you write. For this project you are making a worm book cover.

1. Think about something that would make a good story. Do you like to write stories about animals or people? Do you like to write stories about things that happen to you?

2. Look through the many choices in the Wacky Brush tool options. Use the arrows at the far right side of the screen to look at the many levels. You can find the worm that is used in the example in *Kid Pix Studio*. If you are using *Kid Pix 2* you will need to use the Wacky Pencil to draw a worm.

3. Click on the worm and click on a place near the top of the screen. Drag the mouse diagonally until it is the size that you want. You can write the title of your story on the worm.

4. Use the Typewriter tool or select Type Text from the Goodies menu. Select the font that you want to use from the bottom of the screen. Choose a color that will show when it is printed. Click where you want your title to start and type in your title. Don't forget to type in the name of the author—you.

5. Print your book cover. Select Print from the File menu.

6. Cut out the shape that you made. Use the shape as a pattern and cut out a few pages of blank paper or paper with lines. Staple the book together and write your story.

What Else Can I Do?

1. To make a book about the five senses with a hand-shaped cover, select the Wacky Pencil and put your hand on the screen. Trace around your hand with the Wacky Pencil. Select the Typewriter tool and write the following title for your book cover: The Five Senses.

2. Make shape books about trains, bugs, or any other interesting things.

Simple Projects

Make a Shape Book (cont.)

Simple Projects

Make a Shape Book *(cont.)*

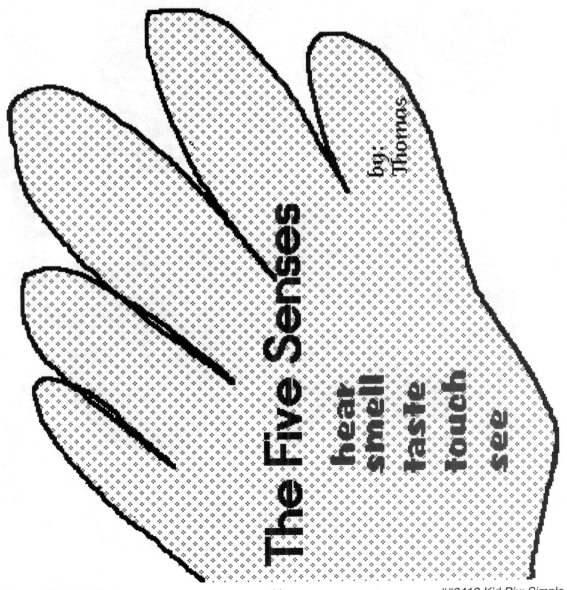

Simple Projects

Make a Shape Book (cont.)

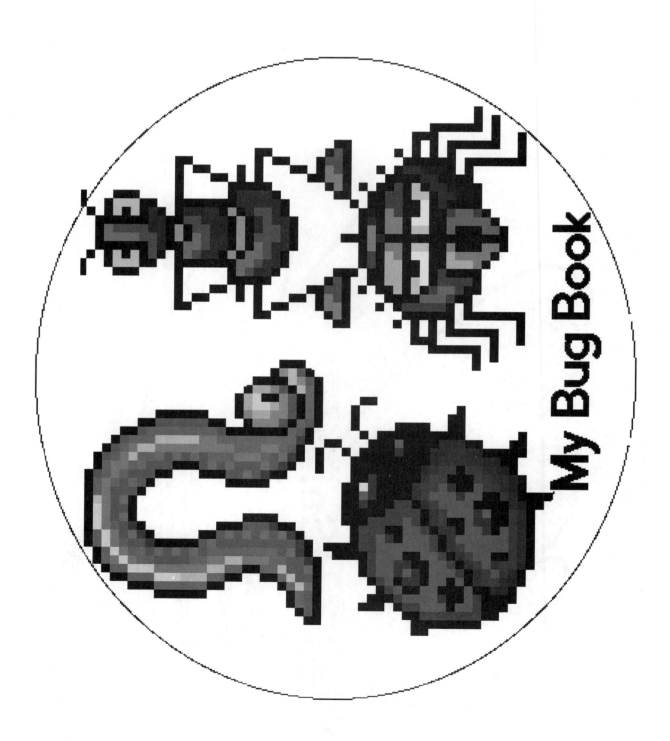

Make a Shape Book (cont.)

Simple Projects

Make a Shape Book (cont.)

#2412 Kid Pix: Simple Projects   14   © Teacher Created Materials, Inc.

Simple Projects

Make a Postcard

This Project

There are many places that we go that we would like to share with someone else. An enjoyable way to share with someone is to send a postcard. With this project you are going to draw a picture for the front of the postcard, paste it onto heavier paper, and then write the message for the postcard. When everything is put together, you can really send the card—with a stamp, of course.

1. Think about what kind of picture that you want to be on the front of your postcard. Is it a picture of you and your house? Is it a picture of somewhere that you have visited? Decide on the picture that you want.

2. Use the Wacky Pencil to draw, the Wacky Brush for special effects, the Rubber Stamps for rubber stamps, and all the *Kid Pix* drawing tools to create your picture. Make sure it is very colorful.

3. Print your postcard using one of the smaller sizes so that it is the size of a postcard. Select Print and one of the smaller sizes of print–size choices.

4. Now it is time to cut out your postcard picture and paste it onto another piece of paper that is thicker. Your teacher might have some paper called "cardstock" for you to use.

Making the Back of the Postcard

5. The back of the postcard is made using the Typewriter tool and the Straight Line tool.

6. Use the Straight Line tool while holding down the shift key and make a line down the center of the screen. This is the line that separates the address from the postcard message.

7. Select the Typewriter tool or select Goodies and choose Type Text. Write your message on the left side of the card. Write the name and address of the person who is getting the postcard on the right side of the card.

Simple Projects

Make a Postcard *(cont.)*

Making the Back of the Postcard *(cont.)*

8. Print the message side in the same size as the picture side. This is very important because you are going to paste the two sides together.

9. Paste the message side of the postcard to the back of the postcard picture you already made. All you need now is a stamp, and you can really mail this card.

What Else Can I Do?

1. You might want to make more postcards for special events in your family, like birthdays and holidays.

2. Pretend that you are a character in a book that you have read and send a postcard with a picture from the book and a message from the character. You might make a picture from *Charlotte's Web* and write a message as if you really were the spider.

3. Maybe you could write a postcard from Amelia Bedelia or from one of the ducks in *Make Way for Ducklings*.

4. An interesting postcard would be one with a picture from an area that you are studying and a message as if you were on vacation there.

#2412 Kid Pix: Simple Projects   16   © Teacher Created Materials, Inc.

Simple Projects

Make a Postcard *(cont.)*

Dear Alexandra,

This a picture of the ship that I was on. It was fun watching the birds swoop down to catch and eat fish.

Love,

Melinda

Alexandra Adams

146 – 28th Avenue

Los Altos, CA. 37560

Simple Projects

Make a Postcard (cont.)

Dear Philip,

I am afraid we will be late. I have been waiting to cross the street for so long.

Love,

Daisy Duck

Philip White
Longview Gardens
326 - Garden Street
Boston, MA. 94685

Simple Projects

A Teepee

This Project

Some Native Americans used teepees for their homes. The teepee was easily folded up and moved to where there was more food for the family and animals. In this project you will make a teepee with Native American designs. When the teepee is finished, you print it and staple it to a paper roll so that it can stand up. If many of your friends make teepees, your classroom could have a village.

1. First, you need to make the teepee outline.

2. Select the Straight Line tool to make the outline of the tent. Do not use the shift key with the Straight Line tool here. Draw the teepee shape as a triangle. Add lines at the top for poles that hold the tent.

3. Decorate the outside of the tent with rubber stamps that would tell about the world of the Native Americans. Select the Rubber Stamp tool and choose stamps of the sun, fish, moon, stars, and water.

4. To make the door to the teepee, select the Oval tool. Click at the top of the doorway and drag down to the bottom of the teepee.

5. To make it look like the door is open, select the Paint Can tool and the color black. Fill the door with black, and it will look like you can walk right into the teepee. You might want to put a face peeking out of the doorway. Use the Rubber Stamp tool and a face option.

6. When your teepee is finished, print it. Select File and choose Print. Cut out the teepee and glue or staple it to a paper roll.

What Else Can I Do?

Now let's use *Kid Pix* to design the rest of the village.

1. On a new screen, draw some trees. Use the Wacky Pencil, or you can use rubber stamps for the trees. If you need more choices of stamps, select the Goodies menu and choose Pick a Stamp Set.

2. Some interesting trees can be drawn by selecting the Wacky Brush tool and the fractal tree option.

3. Use the Rubber Stamp tool and options to find animals that would be found in a Native American village. You might look for horses, cattle, animals of the desert, or animals that live in or near lakes or streams.

© Teacher Created Materials, Inc.   ##2412 Kid Pix: Simple Projects

Simple Projects

A Teepee (cont.)

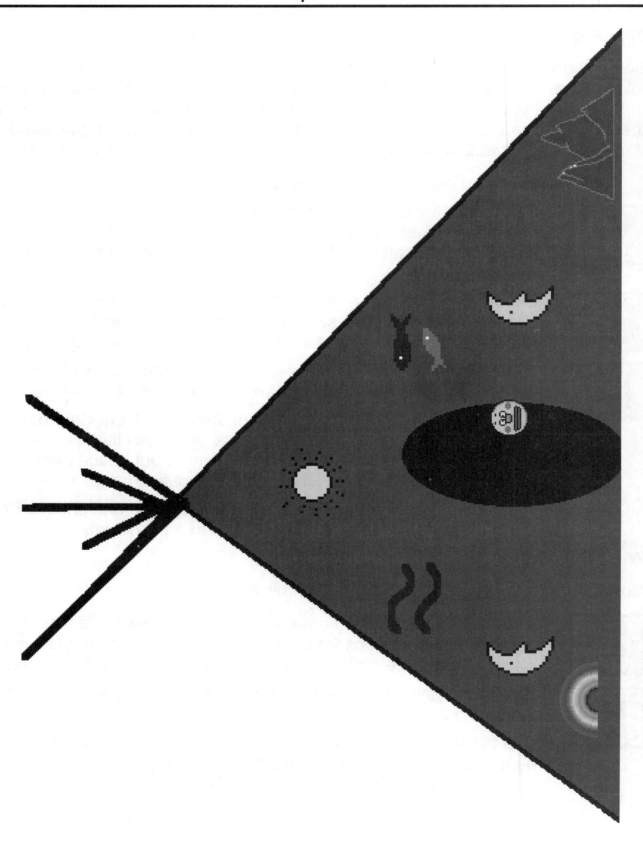

Simple Projects

A Teepee *(cont.)*

Simple Projects

My Own Flashcards

This Project

Sometimes you need to study math facts so that you become faster at doing your math work. As you make your cards, you are practicing those math facts.

1. First, you draw a rectangle on the screen and divide it into three parts.

2. The first two parts are for the problem, and the third part is where you put the answer. After you print the cards, you fold back the answer on the line and glue it down.

3. Select the Rectangle tool and draw a rectangle on the screen near the upper left-hand corner. Select the Straight Line tool and hold down the Shift key as you draw the three lines. Now you have one flashcard.

4. To make the rest of the flashcards, you are going to use the Moving Van tool to copy the first flashcard five more times.

5. Select the Moving Van tool and choose the magnet option on the bottom row. Put your mouse arrow at the upper left side of the rectangle and drag to put the flashing lines around the rectangle. Move the mouse to the center of the rectangle, and you see that the cursor turns into a magnet.

6. Hold down the mouse button and the option key and move the rectangle directly below. You now have another blank flashcard.

7. Repeat steps 5 and 6 again, and you have another flashcard. Keep doing this again and again until you have six flashcards.

8. Select the Rubber Stamp tool and a rubber stamp from the options and, starting from the left, put one or more rubber stamps and then a plus or minus sign. In the next box, put in some more rubber stamps and an equals sign. In the third box put in the answer to the problem. Repeat these steps for all of the flashcards.

9. Print the cards. Cut them out, fold on the line, and then glue the last part to the back of the card. Put the flashcards in an envelope.

What Else Can I Do?

1. Make flashcards for your spelling words.
2. Make a set of flashcards for your vocabulary words.
3. Make a set of flashcards with number words on them.

#2412 Kid Pix: Simple Projects © Teacher Created Materials, Inc.

Simple Projects

My Own Flashcards (cont.)

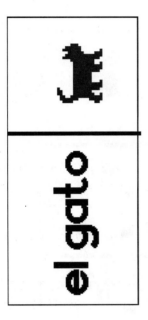
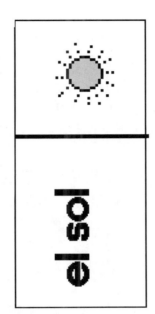
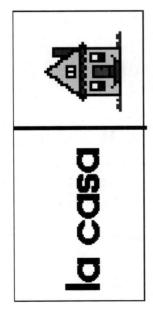
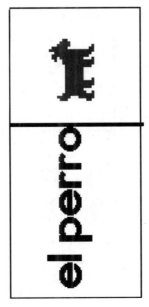

© Teacher Created Materials, Inc. 23 ##2412 Kid Pix: Simple Projects

Simple Projects

My Own Flashcards (cont.)

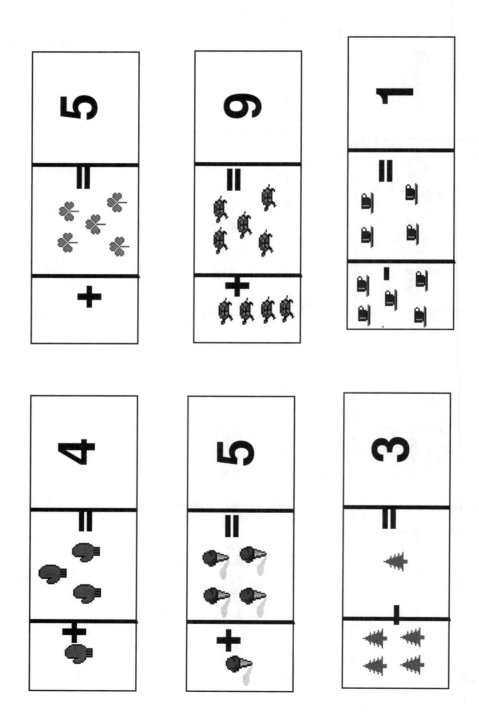

Simple Projects

Alphabet Code

This Project

Writing to friends in secret code has always been a favorite activity of children around the world. In this project, you are going to use rubber stamps to create an alphabet code.

1. On the screen draw two lines at the top and two lines at the bottom of the screen. Select the Straight Line tool and hold down the shift key as you draw the lines. The first line is for the beginning part of the alphabet to sit on. The second line is for the rubber stamps to sit on. The third line is for part of the alphabet to sit on, and the fourth line is for their matching rubber stamps. The fifth line is for the end of the alphabet, and the sixth line is for the last of the rubber stamps.

2. Now write the alphabet. Select the Typewriter tool or select Goodies and choose Type Text. Click at the first part of the first line and type the letter A. Press the Space Bar three times and then type the letter B.

3. Continue on the first line to the letter J.

4. Now click on the second line and type the letter K. Press the Space Bar three times and type in the letter L. Continue until you finish the line with T.

5. Click on the fifth line and type the letter U. Press the Space Bar three times and type the letter V. Continue on this line until you finish with the letter Z.

6. Now it's time to match the letters to the pictures.

7. Select the Rubber Stamp tool and look through the options to find stamps that match the letters. You might use a flower stamp for "f" and the eye stamp for "e."

8. Stamp the picture on the line below the letter. If there is not a picture to match, draw a small picture with the Wacky Pencil and use the Paint Can to fill it in.

9. When you are finished, print your alphabet code.

10. You can write secret messages to friends on the screen. To read your secret messages, all they need to do is to look at your alphabet code paper.

© Teacher Created Materials, Inc.   ##2412 Kid Pix: *Simple Projects*

Simple Projects

Alphabet Code (cont.)

What Else Can I Do?

1. Figure out other kinds of codes.

2. Write the alphabet on the screen and then erase the vowels: a, e, i, o, and u. In place of the vowels, put numbers.

For example: 1 b c d 2 f g h 3 j k l m n 4 p q r s t 5 v w x y z

Here is a sentence with this code:

3t 3s r13n3ng. H3, fr32nd.

_ _   _ _   _ _ _ _ _ _ _.

_ _, _ _ _ _ _ _.

#2412 Kid Pix: Simple Projects   26   © Teacher Created Materials, Inc.

Alphabet Code (cont.)

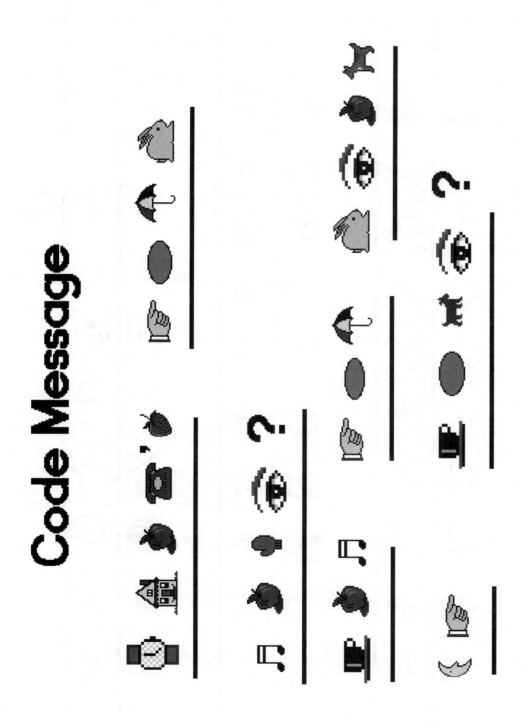

Simple Projects

Alphabet Code (cont.)

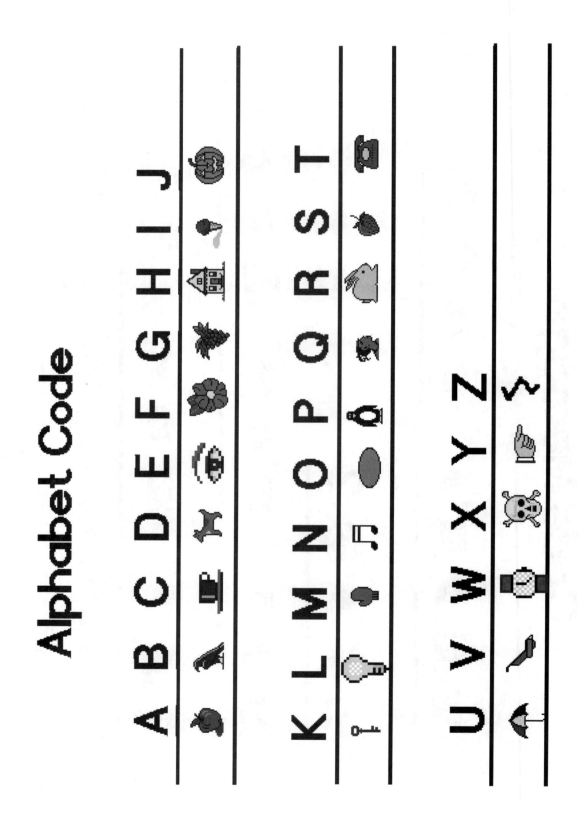

#2412 Kid Pix: Simple Projects   28   © Teacher Created Materials, Inc.

Simple Projects

An Action Picture

This Project

There is so much happening all around us. In school, in your house, at the store, and at the zoo, things are moving all the time. In this project, you are going to make a picture showing action in a place. After your picture is finished, you are going to write action words for your picture. For this example you will see the action at a zoo.

1. First put the animals into the picture. Select the Rubber Stamp tool and use the arrows on the option line to go through the levels of pictures to find some zoo animals. You can find more rubber stamps by selecting Goodies from the menu bar and choosing Pick a Stamp Set. When you see all the choices of stamps on the screen, double-click on the group that you would like to see.

2. Place your animals in different areas on the screen. The birds should be together and the water animals together.

3. After you have placed your animals on the screen, it is time to make them comfortable with the things they need. Use the Wacky Pencil to draw tree branches for the birds and water for the animals that need to be in the water.

4. To make hay for some animals to eat, select the Wacky Brush. Select the hay option from the brush options to make wavy lines that look like hay.

5. Did you draw something you didn't mean to draw? Remember that you can select the Eraser tool and the small eraser options to erase any areas.

6. Now it's time to write the action words for your picture.

7. Select the Typewriter tool or choose Type Text from the Goodies menu. Choose a font, click below the picture, and write the action word for each animal.

8. Use the Typewriter tool to write a title for your picture. You might want to call it "Action at the Zoo."

9. Print your picture. Select Print from the File menu.

What Else Can I Do?

1. Make an action picture of your neighborhood. Put many people in your picture so that you can tell their actions.
2. Make an action picture of your school playground.

© Teacher Created Materials, Inc.

An Action Picture (cont.)

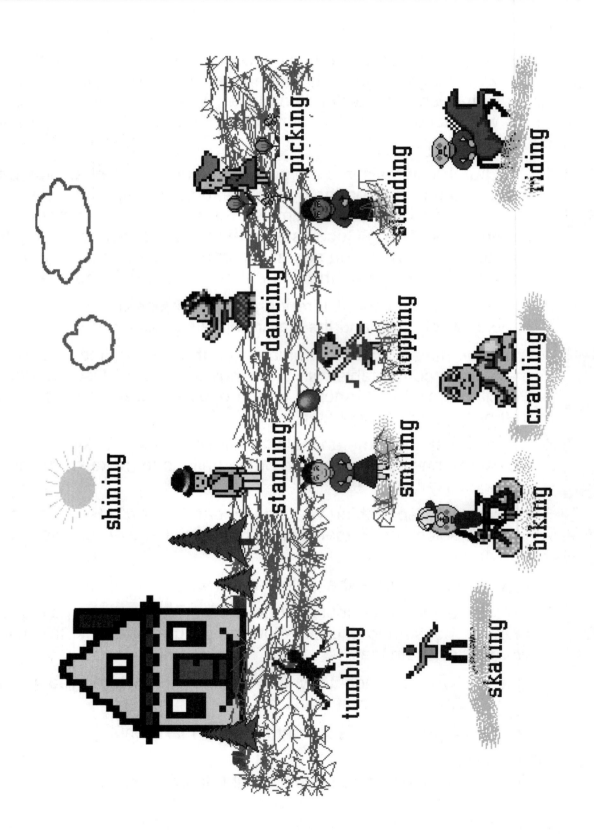

Simple Projects

An Action Picture (cont.)

Simple Projects

Make a Puzzle

This Project

It's really fun to create your own puzzle. All you have to do is make a wonderful picture, print it, and cut it apart. Ask your teacher for an envelope in which you can keep your pieces. If your teacher has some heavy paper that can go through the printer, it would be good to use for a puzzle. For this example you will make a puzzle with a picture from the story of the three bears.

1. To draw the picture, start by placing on the screen one of the houses where a bear lives. Select the Rubber Stamp tool and look for a house to use. For more choices, select Goodies and choose Pick a Stamp Set. To make the house large, hold down the shift key or the Option and shift keys while you stamp the picture on the screen.

2. To put the three bears in the picture, select Rubber Stamps and choose the bear. To make three different sizes of bears, use the Shift and Option keys. To make the biggest bear, hold down the Shift, Option, and Control keys if you are using a Mac. If you are using a Windows machine, hold down the shift and Control keys. To make the medium-sized bear, hold down the shift and Option keys while you stamp the bear.

3. Now put some trees and flowers into your picture. To find many kinds of trees, select the Rubber Stamp tool options. You can grow your own tree by selecting Wacky Brush and then the tree option. Click on the screen where you want your tree to grow and watch what happens. You can choose any color for your tree. Hold down the shift key if you want a really large tree.

4. Use the Wacky Pencil to draw any parts that you need. You can use the Wacky Pencil with a color to draw clothes on the bears.

5. If you want to show Goldilocks in the picture, select Rubber Stamps and find a stamp of a girl that looks like Goldilocks. To make the hair golden, you only need to use the Paint Can tool with a yellow color and click in the area of the hair.

6. Remember that you can select the Eraser tool and the small eraser option to erase any areas.

7. Use the Typewriter tool to write a title for your picture, if you want.

Simple Projects

Make a Puzzle *(cont.)*

This Project *(cont.)*

8. Select the Typewriter tool or choose Type Text from the Goodies menu. Choose a font, click below the picture, and write the title.

9. Print your picture. Select Print from the File menu.

10. Cut apart your picture into jigsaw pieces and put them into an envelope for a friend to put together.

What Else Can I Do?

1. Make another puzzle to share with friends and family.

2. Choose a theme for your puzzle. Do you want it to be about animals or people? Do you want your puzzle to be a picture telling about a book that you have read or a story that has been read to you? Do you want your puzzle to be about people who work in your community?

© Teacher Created Materials, Inc. ##2412 Kid Pix: Simple Projects

Simple Projects

Make a Puzzle (cont.)

#2412 Kid Pix: Simple Projects · 34 · © Teacher Created Materials, Inc.

Make a Puzzle (cont.)

Simple Projects

City–Country?

This Project

Some people live in cities, and some live in the country. In the country there is more land around the houses than in the cities. You are going to make pictures of two types of houses, one city house and one country house. Try to choose two types of houses that are really different.

1. How does the house you live in look? Why are some houses in the world made of straw? Why are some houses made of brick or wood? What are some things that people have to think about before they build a house?

2. Select the Straight Line tool, hold down the shift key and draw a line down the middle of the screen. On the right side of the screen, you will draw a country picture and on the left side, a city picture.

3. Select the Wacky Brush tool and use the arrow at the right to get to the level where you see bricks and logs. If you are using *Kid Pix* 2, you will need to use the Straight Line tool and shift key to draw houses. You might use the Rectangle tool and use the Fill option.

4. Select the logs or bricks, hold down the mouse button, and pull diagonally to build a house. You can click and place the logs or bricks one by one. Click individually to place logs or bricks in empty spaces.

5. To add a roof, select the roof icon and click and pull diagonally to place it. You can use the eraser here also.

6. To make windows and a door, select the Rectangle tool and the color white from the Color Palette. Click at the top of where you want the door or window and drag diagonally.

7. Now select the Rubber Stamp tool and choose rubber stamps and use drawing tools to finish your picture.

8. For the city side of your picture, you can select rubber stamps to build the house. Select the rubber stamp that you want (there are apartment houses in the original group of rubber stamps that you can use). Hold down the shift and/or option keys to make the stamps larger. You could also build your house using the Straight Line tool and other tools.

9. Now use the Straight Line tool and the color black to draw streets. Use the rubber stamps to add other things that you find in a city.

City–Country? (cont.)

What Else Can I Do?

Now you can add a title to each part of the picture.

1. Select the Typewriter Tool from the menu. If you are using the older version of *Kid Pix*, select Goodies and then Type Text. Click on the screen where you want your title to be and type in the words. You might want to title one side "City" and the other side "Country."

2. You can create other homes where people live. Find the igloo in the rubber stamps and make an icy picture.

3. Find some rubber stamps that show what the area is like near the igloo.

4. Select Goodies and Type Text to write about the land where igloos are used for housing.

5. You will find some interesting houses in the Hodge Podge choice in rubber stamps. Select the Rubber Stamp tool, select Goodies, and then choose the group of stamps that has houses in it.

Simple Projects

City–Country? *(cont.)*

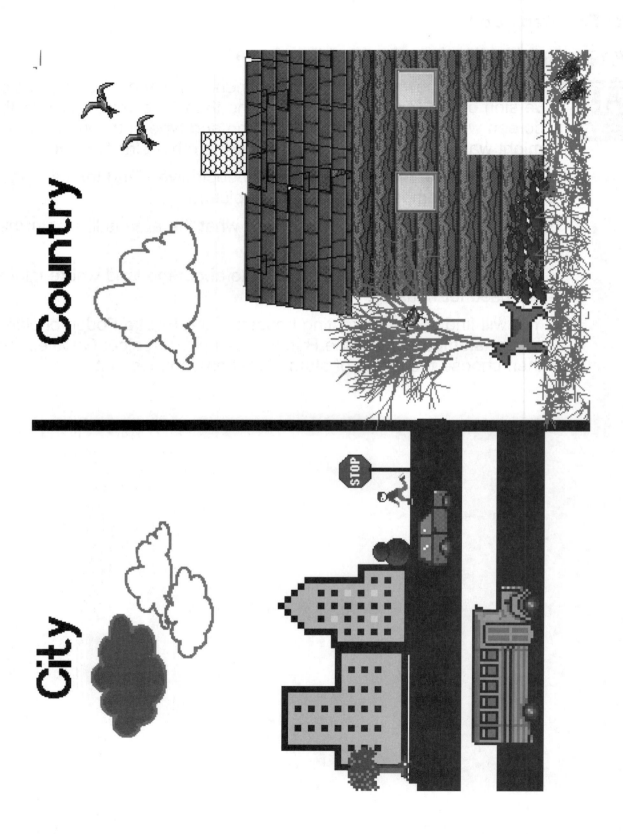

City–Country? (cont.)

Simple Projects

Put All the Eggs in the Basket

This Project basket—on the computer

In the spring many people celebrate the blooming of the flowers and the birth of baby animals. Some people celebrate by coloring eggs and putting them in a basket. You are going to make some colored eggs and put them in a basket—on the computer. When the basket is full, print your picture, cut it out, and staple it to a container you can use to put eggs, candy, etc., in.

1. First, you make the basket. Select the Wacky Pencil and draw a big basket on the screen. Choose a happy spring color for the basket.

2. Now it's time to put your eggs in the basket. There are two ways to make the eggs for the basket.

- Select the Oval tool, select a color, and select a texture from the choices at the bottom of the screen. Click where you want your egg to be and drag to the size you want it.

- Select the Oval tool and draw an egg with just an outline. This is done by choosing from the bottom of the screen the texture pattern that just shows an outline of the oval. Draw the egg.

- Select the Paint Can tool. From the options at the bottom of the screen, select a fill and a color that you like for your egg. Click in the middle of the egg, and there is your decorated egg. Remember, if you don't like it, click on the Undo Man and the fill goes away. You can now choose another fill.

3. Be sure to put some eggs in the bottom of the basket too.

4. After you have placed all your eggs in the basket, it is time to add decorations to them. Select the Rubber Stamp tool and choose stamps to decorate the eggs.

5. Your eggs are in the basket, and now you can finish the basket. You are going to draw some lines on the basket to make the eggs look like they are really inside a basket. If you draw your lines over the eggs, it makes them look like they are in the basket.

6. Fill in the empty areas of the basket, using the Paint Can with a nice light color. Click on the Paint Can and a color and click in each empty area. Be sure the tip of the paint coming out of the can is in the empty area. Use the Undo Man to take away what you do not want.

#2412 Kid Pix: Simple Projects   © Teacher Created Materials, Inc.

Put All the Eggs in the Basket (cont.)

This Project basket—on the computer (cont.)

7. Print your eggs-in-a-basket picture. Cut out the basket and staple it to a container. Using a container, you can put some candy eggs in it and attach a handle made from colored paper.

What Else Can I Do?

1. Use the Typewriter tool and write your friends' names on three eggs.

2. Maybe your teacher would like to make a bulletin board using everyone's baskets.

3. Make a special basket for a special person, decorating the eggs in his or her favorite colors.

Simple Projects

Put All the Eggs in the Basket (cont.)

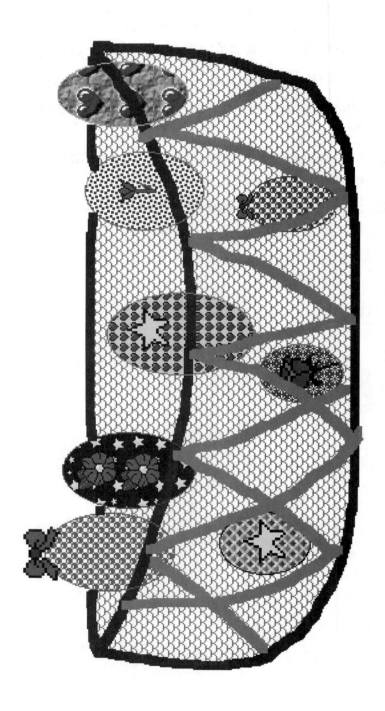

#2412 Kid Pix: Simple Projects 42 © Teacher Created Materials, Inc.

Elephant Valentines

This Project

One of the favorite special days for people everywhere is Valentine's Day. Even elephants like Valentine's Day. You are going to make an elephant valentine to give to your favorite person or favorite elephant.

1. First, you need to make a dot near the top of the screen and a dot straight down from it near the bottom of the screen. Choose the color red. Select the Oval tool and hold down the shift key. Click on the screen and drag just a tiny bit to make a small dot.

2. Use the Wacky Pencil and color red and start at the top dot and connect to the bottom dot, making ½ a heart. Now do the same thing on the other side.

3. Using the Wacky Pencil, draw the elephant trunk and then the feet in red. Choose black to draw the eye, ear, and mouth. You can add any other decorations that you want.

4. Select the Paint Can and a red color and click in the middle of the elephant heart to fill it.

5. Print your valentine, cut it out, and give it to someone you like.

6. If you want to use this picture as part of a greeting card, use the Typewriter tool to write a greeting. You might want to write the following:

My Valentine

To My Valentine

Love

A Trunk Full of Wishes

Simple Projects

Elephant Valentines *(cont.)*

What Else Can I Do?

Use your imagination to create other animal valentines.

1. You might want to make other valentine animals or people.

2. Draw the heart just the way that you did for the elephant but turn it in different directions. Look at the examples for ideas.

3. A fun valentine can be found in the Wacky Brush options in *Kid Pix Studio.* Select Wacky Brush and then use the arrows at the bottom to find the Option line that has the heart in the middle. Click in the upper part of the screen and drag the heart to fill the screen. If you want to add a speech bubble, use the arrows to move down through the options until you find the speech bubble you want. Click on the screen and drag to the size you want. You might want to use the Wacky Pencil to draw in your own speech bubbles.

4. To write inside the speech bubble, select the Typewriter tool or Type Text in the Goodies menu, click inside the bubble, and type.

5. Print the valentine and give it to a friend.

#2412 Kid Pix: Simple Projects 44 © *Teacher Created Materials, Inc.*

Elephant Valentines (cont.)

Elephant Valentines (cont.)

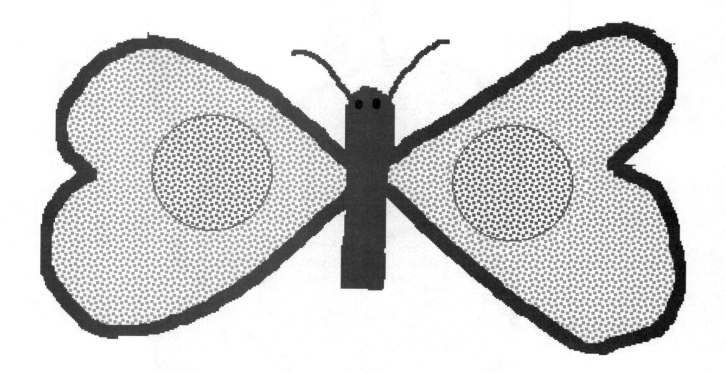

Elephant Valentines *(cont.)*

Simple Projects

Elephant Valentines (cont.)

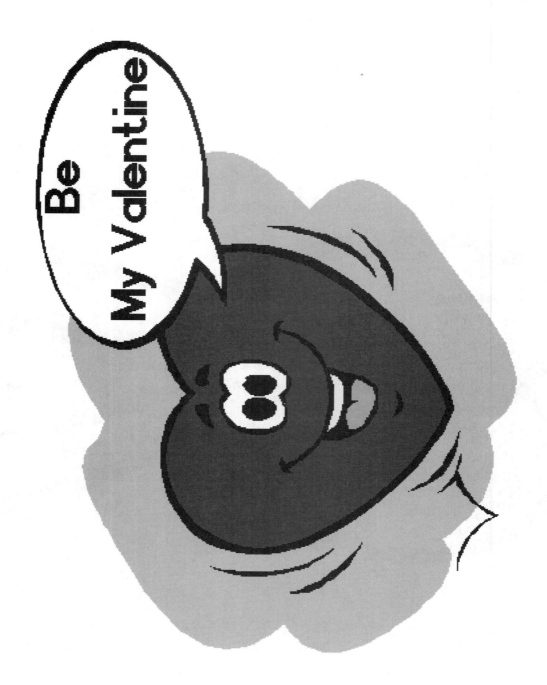

#2412 Kid Pix: Simple Projects

Simple Projects

My Own Game Board

This Project

Making games for you and your friends to play is fun and easy to do.

1. First you make a game board, and then you have fun playing the game. Think about the theme of your game board. Why not make your game theme something that you really like. Do you like animals, cars, bright colors, trains, or food?

2. Select the Straight Line tool and hold down the shift key to make the game board form. Start at the upper left–hand corner and draw a straight line to the other side of the screen. Go down the right side, using the Straight Line tool and the shift key. Now make a line to connect to that line going across the bottom.

3. Keep using the Straight Line tool and shift key to make lines just under the first one you drew.

4. Now you make the lines for the boxes on your game board. Use the Straight Line tool and hold down the shift key and draw lines making the boxes.

5. Decorate the boxes on the game board with rubber stamps that fit your theme.

6. Use the Typewriter tool or go to Goodies and select Type Text to write directions on your game board. You will need to choose one of the smaller fonts from the bottom of the screen. You might want to write some directions like the following:

   Go 2 spaces.
   Go back 1 space.
   Roll again.
   Lose 1 turn.
   Take 1 more turn.

7. Click in the box and write the directions.

8. Decorate the game board now. Select the Rubber Stamp tool and choose some graphics to decorate the board.

9. Use the Typewriter tool to type in a name for your game.

© Teacher Created Materials, Inc.   49   ##2412 Kid Pix: Simple Projects

Simple Projects

My Own Game Board *(cont.)*

This Project *(cont.)*

10. You might want to use the Paint Can tool and choose some colors to fill the squares. It makes the board look attractive.
11. Print your game board. If your teacher has a heavy paper like card–stock, ask if you can print your game on that paper. You might also paste it on heavy paper or on a file folder.

What Else Can I Do?

Make other game boards for the classroom and for your home.

1. Make a game board in another shape.
2. Make a game board with another theme.

My Own Game Board (cont.)

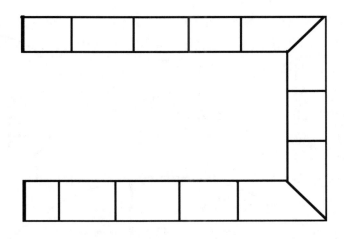

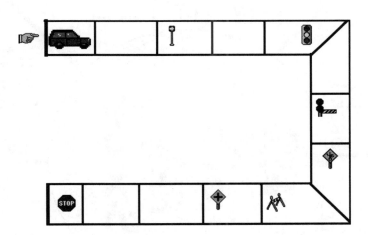

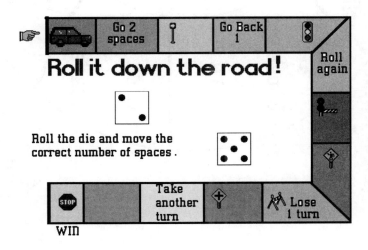

Simple Projects

My Own Game Board (cont.)

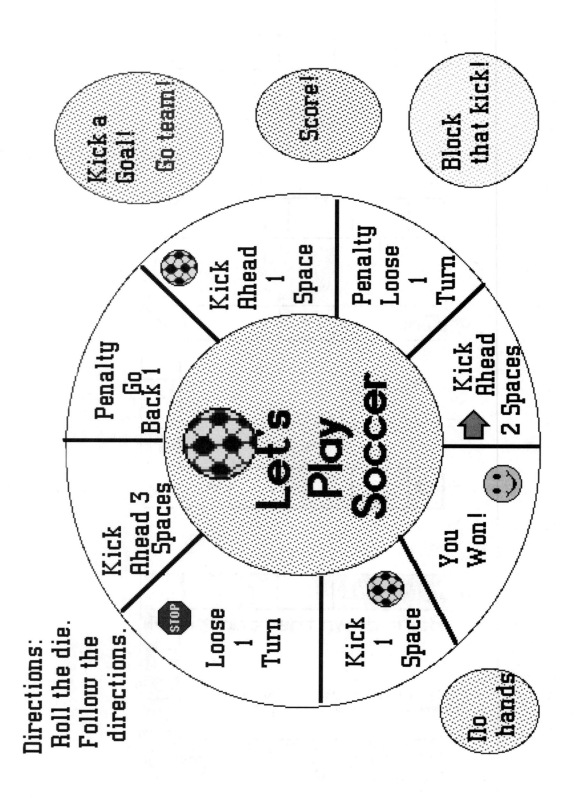

Simple Projects

My Own Game Board (cont.)

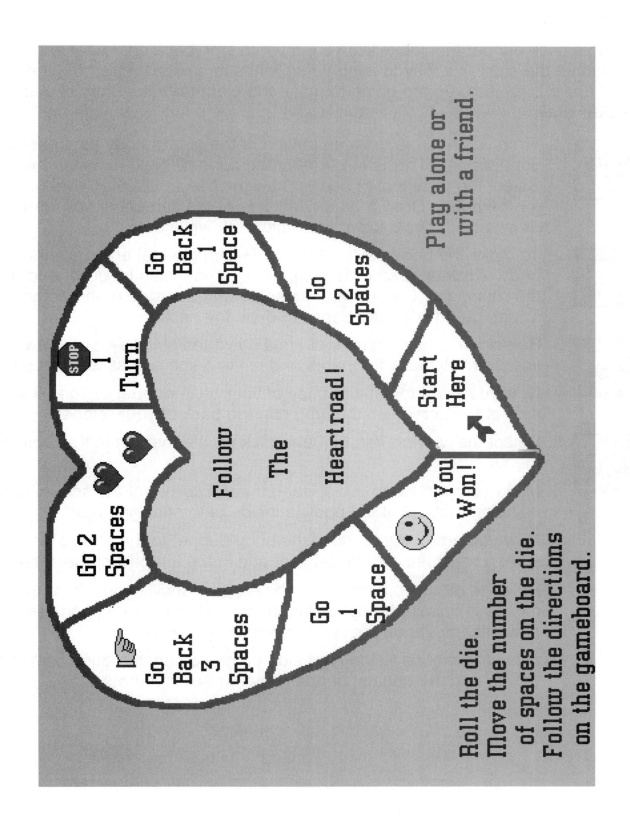

Simple Projects

Puppet People

This Project

Making a stick puppet that looks like your favorite storybook character and using it to act out the story is a way to keep your friends interested in hearing the story. For this project you are going to make the giant from the story of *Jack and the Beanstalk*.

1. First, you need to draw an outline of the giant's body as a base for your puppet. This is the front of the puppet. Next draw the head. Select the Oval tool to use to draw the head. Draw an oval or circle for the head. Draw it on the left side of the screen. If you want to draw a circle, hold down the option key while drawing.

2. To make the body part, select the Rectangle tool and draw the body. Click under the head to the left and a little bit down and drag the rectangle. Draw a thin rectangle on each side of the body for arms. Use the Wacky Pencil to draw the neck.

3. Select the Straight Line tool, hold down the shift key, and draw a line down to make the pants and make a line across for the belt.

4. Now you need to make a copy of your base puppet on the other side of the screen so that you can the back of your puppet.

5. Select the Moving Van tool and click on the magnet in the Option menu.

6. Move your mouse to the upper left-hand corner of the screen and pull diagonally until the body is inside of the flashing box.

7. Now you are going to move the body puppet to the other side of the screen while leaving the original one in the left part of the screen.

8. Hold the mouse button down (the magnet shows you where the mouse is). Hold the option key down. (Holding the option key down keeps the original puppet where you drew it.)

9. Move the mouse to the right side of the screen; the body comes with it, and the original puppet stays where you drew it.

Simple Projects

Puppet People *(cont.)*

What Else Can I Do?

Now it's time to add the clothes to dress the puppet.

1. Select the Wacky Pencil and choose one of the small or medium line widths to draw in the clothes. Draw the shirt and shoes. You can also just leave the outline for the clothes.
2. Draw the same outline of the clothes on the puppet on the right side of the screen but remember that it is the back of the puppet.
3. Select the Paint Can tool and choose a fill pattern from the Options at the bottom of the screen. Click in the middle of the piece of clothing that you want to fill.
4. Select the Rubber Stamp tool and choose a rubber stamp that you would like to add to the clothes to create patterns and designs on the clothes.
5. To fill in the skin color, use the Paint Can and choose a color for the skin.

6. A fun way to draw hair is to use the Wacky Brush and the hay option. Select the correct color for your hair. Hold down the option key as you draw to make the hair thicker.
7. Be sure that the back of your puppet matches the front.
8. Print the puppet page.
9. Cut out the two puppets and glue them onto a tongue depressor or craft stick.
10. Now make puppets for your favorite storybook characters, using all the directions.

© Teacher Created Materials, Inc. ##2412 Kid Pix: Simple Projects

Simple Projects

Puppet People (cont.)

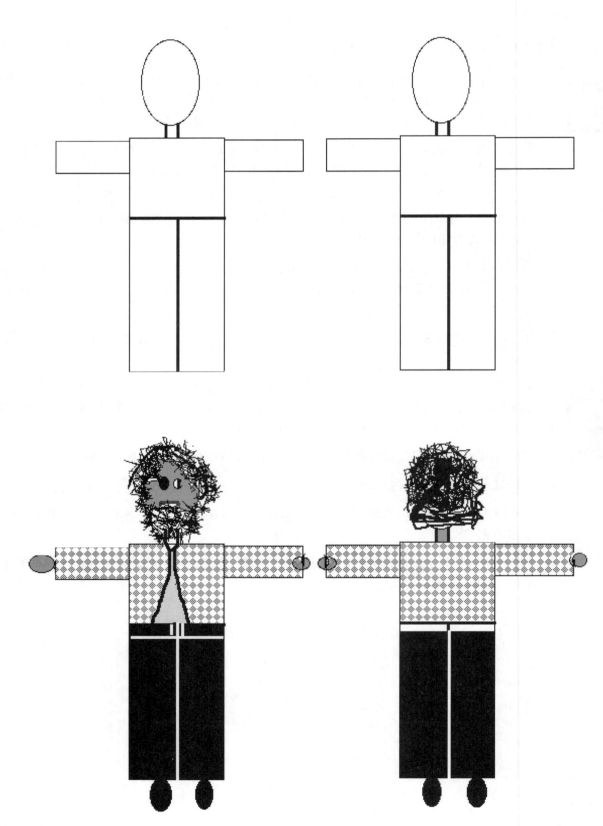

#2412 Kid Pix: Simple Projects   56   © Teacher Created Materials, Inc.

Simple Projects

Fun Writing

This Project

It's fun to write with all different kinds of writing tools. In school you usually write with pencils. You are now going to write with all kinds of tools in *Kid Pix*.

1. First, use the Wacky Pencil. Select the Wacky Pencil and then choose the question mark option at the bottom of the screen. Write your name, using the colors. Now choose a thicker line width and write your name again.

2. Now select the Wacky Brush tool and look for the bubbles option. Write your name in bubbles. You can choose a new color and write it again. Try writing each letter of your name in a different color.

3. Use other options from the Wacky Brush tool options menu and write your name again.

4. Try to write your name with the alphabet option from the Wacky Brush tool. If you are using *Kid Pix Studio*, try using the bugs in the Wacky Brush options to write your name.

5. Select the Rectangle tool and make a solid rectangle on the screen. Now select the Eraser tool and the color white and choose one of the small erasers from the left side of the screen. Write your name with the eraser in the solid rectangle.

6. Select the Oval tool and the question mark option and draw an oval on the screen. Use the Eraser tool with the white color and a small-size eraser to carve your name.

7. When you have filled the screen with your name, select Print from the File menu and print your name page.

What Else Can I Do?

1. Write the names of your friends, using all the fun writing tools. Use the Typewriter tool to title your picture. You might want to write "My Friends" at the top of the page.

2. Write the names of your family, using the different writing tools. Title this page "My Family."

3. Write your spelling words, in different styles. Writing your spelling words will help you to learn them.

Simple Projects

Fun Writing (cont.)

Fun Writing (cont.)

Simple Projects

Fun Writing *(cont.)*

#2412 Kid Pix: Simple Projects © Teacher Created Materials, Inc.

Pinwheels

This Project

Pinwheels move when the wind pushes their edges. When the pinwheel turns, you see beautiful colors moving and swirling.

1. In this project you are going to make a pinwheel that really works. The pinwheel is your own personal design. This makes it very special. When it is finished, take it into the wind and watch it turn.

2. Design the pinwheel first.

3. Since the pinwheel has to be perfectly square, you need to draw a square first on the screen. Select the Rectangle tool first and hold down the shift key as you draw a square on the screen.

4. After the square is drawn on the screen, you can put your design inside of it.

5. You can select Paint Can and a fill option for an overall design.

6. You might choose a Rubber Stamp option and stamp all over the square.

7. When your pinwheel design is finished, print it.

8. You need to use a ruler now. Turn the pinwheel over so the design side is down. Draw four straight lines from the four corners to the center. You need to leave a square of space in the center of the pinwheel.

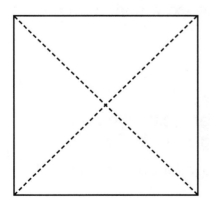

Draw these lines to the center.

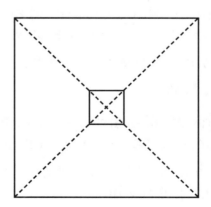

Draw this square in the center.

Simple Projects

Pinwheels *(cont.)*

This Project *(cont.)*

9. Use scissors to cut the four straight lines.

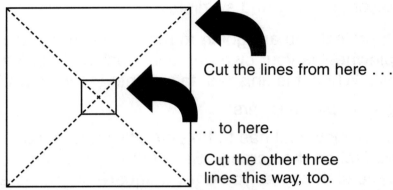

Cut the lines from here . . .

. . . to here.

Cut the other three lines this way, too.

10. Take a corner of the pinwheel to the center of the pinwheel and glue, staple, or tape it. Now do that to every other corner. The corners to be brought in are marked for you.

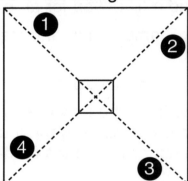

Fold and glue these corners to the center.

11. Make a hole in the center of the pinwheel, through all four folded-down and glued corners. Now tack your pinwheel center to a stick or straw with a tack or small nail. Leave some extra space on the tack or nail so that the pinwheel can turn.

12. Now go "run with the wind."

What Else Can I Do?

1. Think of different types of patterns that you can use in your design. There are some really fun fills if you are using *Kid Pix Studio*.

2. Set many of the pinwheels out on the school grounds in a row and watch them whirl.

Pinwheels (cont.)

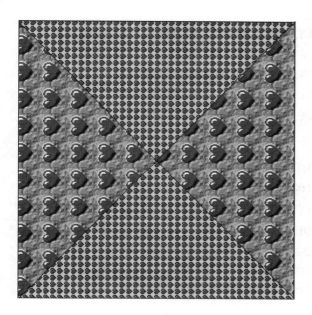

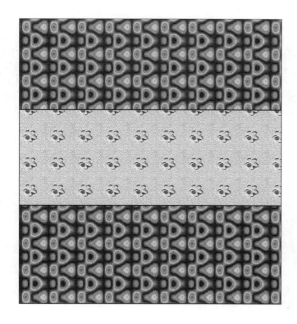
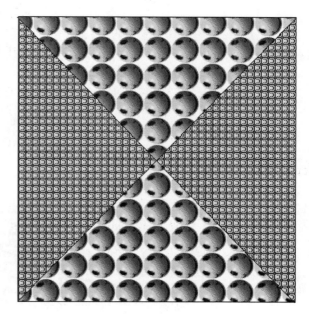

Two Kids–One Computer

This section of *Kid Pix Projects* contains projects that can be done with two students using *Kid Pix* and only one computer. A very common practice, in both computer labs and in classrooms, is to have two students work on the computer together. Whether this is by choice or by circumstance, nonetheless, it is reality.

All of these activities in this section are both fun and educational for students. The focus is on visual memory, patterning, visual discrimination, and interpersonal relationships. There are two activities per page. Duplicate and laminate these pages and place them adjacent to the computer. You'll find students have to attend to what is written on the page in order to complete the activity successfully.

Have students rotate being Partner One or Partner Two.

#2412 Kid Pix: Simple Projects 64 © Teacher Created Materials, Inc.

Hidden Letters

Partner One

- Write your name, letters, or a short sentence on the screen. Use the Typewriter Tool or Type Text from the Goodies menu to do this.

Partner Two

- Look away while your partner writes a word or short sentence.

Partner One

- Select the Rubber Stamp tool and fill the screen with rubber stamps. Use the Wacky Brush and Wacky Brush options for fun designs. Use the Paint Can tool and choose colorful fills.

Partner Two

- Look at the screen to find the word or sentence that Partner One wrote. Look carefully through all the rubber stamps and other options to find it.

Two Kids—One Computer

Remember?

Partner One

- Draw a grid on the screen with six sections. Use the Rectangle Tool and then the Straight Line tool and a medium width.
- Remember that to make a straight line you have to press the shift key while you are drawing.
- Click on the screen and drag diagonally to make the rectangle. Use the Straight Line tool to make the lines.
- Select the Rubber Stamp tool and put a different stamp into each box. Make the stamp larger by holding down the shift key while stamping.

Partner Two

- Look at the grid for ten seconds

Partner One

- Using the Eraser tool, erase the grid.

Partner Two

- Do you remember how the grid looked? Draw the grid and put the correct rubber stamps in it.

#2412 Kid Pix: Simple Projects

Two Kids—One Computer

Where Did It Go?

Partner One

- Make a grid on the screen. Use the Rectangle tool and the Straight Line tool, holding the shift key down.

Partner Two

- Look away from the screen while your partner makes the grid.

Partner One

- Put a rubber stamp in each box.

Partner Two

- Look at the grid and memorize where each of the rubber stamps is placed.

Partner One

- Use the Moving Van tool and move all of the objects to a corner of the screen.

- Select the Moving Van tool and the magnet from the options menu. Click above the rubber stamp and move the lines around the object. Put your mouse in the middle of the object and move it to where you want it to be.

Partner Two

- Use the Moving Van tool to bring all of the objects back to the places where they belong.

Two Kids—One Computer

Erase a Shape

Partner One

- Place many shapes and rubber stamps on the screen. Use the whole screen and many colors. Select the Rectangle tool and the Rubber Stamps tool and choose interesting shapes and stamps.

Partner Two

- Look away from the screen until your partner tells you to look. When ready, look at the screen for ten seconds. Now look away again.

Partner One

- Select the Eraser tool and use one of the small erasers to erase some of the rubber stamps or shapes. When you have erased some of the shapes and rubber stamps, tell your partner to look at the screen.

Partner Two

- Name the things that were erased.

To make it really much harder, have Partner Two put back the items that were erased. Wow!

Two Kids—One Computer

What's Wrong with This Picture?

Partner One

- Draw a picture on the screen that has some things wrong in it.
- You might draw a tree with strange colors or put on the tree fruit that doesn't really grow there.
- You might put rubber stamps of animals on the screen and use the Eraser tool to take away some of their body parts.
- Be very clever and keep some of the changes very small to fool your partner.

Partner Two

- Your job is to look carefully at the picture that your partner has drawn on the screen and figure out what is wrong with it. Use the Eraser tool and erase the wrong things and then put in the right things. You may need to use the Wacky Pencil to draw in some animal legs and tails.

© Teacher Created Materials, Inc.   69   ##2412 Kid Pix: Simple Propjects

Two Kids—One Computer

Tell Me What to Draw

Partner One

- Sit at the computer and listen to the directions given by your partner. Your partner is going to tell you how to draw a picture of yourself.

Partner Two

- Tell your partner exactly what tools to use and how to use them. For example: "Choose the Oval tool and click in the middle of the screen. Drag the tool and stop now."

Partner One

- Continue to follow the directions of your partner until there is a picture of you on the screen.

Copy My Picture

Partner One

- Draw a line down the center of the screen. Use the Straight Line tool and be sure to hold down the shift key as you draw the line.
- Now on one side of the line create a picture, using the *Kid Pix* tools.

Partner Two

- Your job is to create an exact copy of your partner's picture on the blank side of the screen. How closely does your picture match?

Two Kids—One Computer

Connect the Shapes

Partner One

- You are the artist in this activity. Listen to directions from your partner who will tell you what shapes to draw. Try to make a picture with the different shapes.

Partner Two

- Tell your partner different shapes and have your partner draw them on the screen. Tell the colors your partner should use also.

- When your partner says that there is an object or picture on the screen—stop.

- Connect all the shapes, using the Wacky Pencil. Is there really a picture that you recognize?

Two Kids—One Computer

Where's My Tail?

Partner One

- Draw an elephant on the screen. Use the Wacky Pencil to draw the elephant and use the Paint Can with a color to fill in the elephant. In the corner of the screen, draw a tail for the elephant.

Partner Two

- When the drawing of the elephant is finished, your job is to move the tail to the elephant.
- Select the Moving Van tool and choose the magnet option.
- Click right above the tail to the far left.
- Drag the box diagonally over the tail.
- Now move to the center of the tail, hold your mouse button down, and move the tail to the right place on the elephant.

© Teacher Created Materials, Inc. ##2412 Kid Pix: Simple Projects

Two Kids—One Computer

Follow Me

Partner One

- Tell your partner that you are going to give directions for drawing an object. The directions will be simple.

- When you tell your partner the directions, have a picture in mind that you really want to be drawn.

- For example: Think of a house and how it looks. Tell your partner: "Select a rectangle and make it medium sized on the screen. Put two smaller rectangles on the larger rectangle. Put another rectangle at the bottom of the large rectangle. Go to the Paint Can tool and choose a fill. Fill the large rectangle."

Partner Two

- Ask your partner what object was thought of when the directions were given. Does it match your drawing?

#2412 Kid Pix: Simple Projects © Teacher Created Materials, Inc.

Picture It!

Partner One

- Place many different rubber stamps on the screen.
- Choose stamps that are hard to link together. You might choose an animal stamp, a rainbow, a ball, and a bow.

Partner Two

- Your job is to link these stamps together in a picture.
- Use the drawing tools and more stamps to make a scene that makes sense out of all the rubber stamps. You are making a scene around them.

Two Kids—One Computer

Make Something from Nothing

Partner One

- Put one or more lines, boxes, or other shapes on the screen.

Partner Two

- Look at what has been placed on the screen by your partner. It is your job to make a picture from these lines and shapes.
- Could the two boxes be connected and decorated to make a train? Can you make an animal from the lines on the screen?

Partner One

- Write a sentence on the screen, describing the picture made by your partner.
- Use the Typewriter tool or Type Text in the Goodies menu to write your sentence.

Two Kids—One Computer

Dot-to-Dot Picture

Partner One

- You are going to make a dot-to-dot picture and have your partner connect the dots.
- Select Wacky Brush and the dot-to-dot option.
- Hold down your mouse button and carefully draw a picture on the screen.
- When you are finished and you lift your mouse button, the lines will disappear.
- If you want to control the dot-to-dot more, click each number on the screen as you design a picture.

Partner Two

- It is your job to connect the dots.
- Select the Wacky Pencil and the fine line width.
- Hold your mouse button down and starting at one, connect the dots to see what picture your partner has drawn.

© Teacher Created Materials, Inc. ##2412 Kid Pix: Simple Projects

Two Kids—One Computer

Yum Yum—Ice-Cream Sundaes

Partner One

- Select the Rubber Stamp and choose the ice-cream cone option. Your partner is going to add the toppings to the ice-cream cone.

Partner Two

- Your job is to put on the ice cream toppings that will make it taste even better.
- You can use the Oval tool to draw another scoop of ice cream and use the Paint Can tool to add the color to the ice cream.
- Now use the Wacky Brush to find interesting toppings for the ice cream. You might want to use the straw option and a brown color to make a chocolate topping.
- Be creative!

Tic-Tac-Toe

Partner One

- Draw a tic-tac-toe grid on the screen.
- Select the Straight Line tool and hold down the shift key while drawing the grid.
- Now choose a rubber stamp to be your marker.

Partner Two

- Choose a rubber stamp to be your marker.
- Place your marker in one square and then have your partner put the next marker in.
- When there are three in a row, use the Straight Line tool to draw the line through the winning markers.

Two Kids—One Computer

Hangman for Two

Partner One

- Draw the base for the hangman on the screen.
- Put dashes under the hangman where the letters that are to be guessed can be written.

Partner Two

- Use the Typewriter tool to put in a letter that you think is in the word.
- Type the letter at the top of the hangman so you can remember that you chose that letter before.

Partner One

- If your partner types the wrong letter, click on the Undo Man to take away the letter.
- Then use the Wacky Pencil and draw in one part of the man.

Partner Two

- Keep going until your partner has completed the picture of the man or until you have filled in all of the missing letters.

Two Kids—One Computer

Roll It

Partner One

- You are going to roll some dice for your partner, and then your partner will put a number on the die to match the number of dots there.
- Select the Wacky Brush tool and the dice option.
- Click on the screen and a die appears. Now click all over the screen to get many more dice.

Partner Two

- Your job is to count the number of dots on each die and write that number on top of it.
- Select the Typewriter tool or select Type Text from the Goodies menu to use to write your numbers.

© Teacher Created Materials, Inc.   ##2412 Kid Pix: Simple Projects

Tips and Tricks with Kid Pix

These tips and tricks come from many hours of exploring *Kid Pix* with teachers and students. We hope that these save you and your students time and frustration and add to your enjoyment of *Kid Pix*.

Entering Text Hints

1. When using the (T) or text tool to type text, you must click on the screen before you start typing. Often students will select a font and start typing and then call for teacher's help because their typing isn't showing on the screen. Remind them that they must click on the screen first.

2. If you want to change fonts from one sentence or a word to the next, you must click on the screen first or when you change fonts, the previous font will also change.

Drawing Hints

1. Hold down the option or control key when you are trying different Wacky Brush options to make objects larger or fuller.

2. When you choose the Eraser tool, you see the four erasers on the lower left side of the screen. Use any of these erasers as you would the familiar pink eraser. They erase in small segments. The other eraser choices erase the entire screen.

3. In Wacky Brush you can click on the ABC option and make a dot-to-dot alphabet page. To change the alphabet to words so that students can draw pictures with words, go to "Goodies" and select Alphabet Text. The next screen has the alphabet highlights. Type in the words that you want, and when you choose the A-B-C option in Wacky Brush, you can draw with your words.

4. The rubber stamps can be made larger by holding down option, control, shift or alt and control keys, depending on computers.

5. When there are tool options shown at the bottom of the screen, you can find more options by clicking on the arrows at the far right of the option bar.

6. To make the Straight Line tool draw straight, hold down the shift key as you draw. To make the Rectangle tool draw a square, hold down the shift key and to make the Oval tool draw a circle, hold down the shift key.

#2412 Kid Pix: Simple Projects 82 © *Teacher Created Materials, Inc.*

Tips and Tricks with Kid Pix *(cont.)*

7. If you click on the ? option to get multicolors for using with the Rectangle, Oval, or other drawing tools, return to a single color by clicking on the desired texture and then the color.

8. The Eye Dropper tool is a useful option to use when you need to match a color that you have used previously. Click on the Eyedropper tool and then click on the color on the screen that you want to duplicate. The Eyedropper changes to that color. Now use the Paint Can or other tools, and they will be in that color.

Moving Objects and Text Hints

1. If you need to move an object to another location on the screen, click on the Moving Van and the magnet option. Encircle the object with the flashing lines. This means that the object is highlighted and can now be moved. Move the cursor to the middle and move the object to where you want it.

2. If you want to copy the object and leave the original one where it is, hold down the Option key as you move the object.

Editing Stamps Hint

1. If students are using the Edit Stamp option, be sure to tell them to click on Restore Original after they place their stamp. They stamp the edited stamp and then return to the Edit Stamp option and click on Restore Original.

2. Most times when the program is being closed down, there will be a dialog box asking if they want to save the edited stamps. They must click "NO."

Printing Hints

1. You can print in either Portrait or Landscape mode with *Kid Pix*. To change to a mode different from the default (the mode the program is set to, select Options from the Print dialog menu and choose Portrait or Landscape mode. When you print your project, it will be in the mode you chose.

2. You can print in four different sizes. Have students try printing in one of the smallest sizes to make fun tiny books.

© Teacher Created Materials, Inc.   *##2412 Kid Pix: Simple Projects*

Kid Pix Projects Templates

Note to Teachers:

The following directions can be given orally to younger students or can be duplicated and made into a task cards for older or more advanced students. Just photocopy the instructions on cardstock or copy them on regular paper and then glue them onto cardstock.

After students complete the template, they can choose Print from the File menu to print their work.

If you want students to save their work, they need to name it something other than what it is originally titled. It is easiest to have them add their initials to the title. The procedure would be to choose "Save As" from the file menu, type in their initials after the title, and then click Save.

Animal Venn Diagram

Open the Animal Venn Diagram template. Look at all the animals at the bottom of the screen. Think about which animals walk and which animals swim. You are going to move the animals that swim to the circle that says "SWIM." The animals that walk get moved to the circle that says "WALK." Select the Moving Van tool and the magnet option. Move your mouse arrow to the upper part of the picture, click, and then drag the mouse diagonally until you make a circle around the animal. Hold down the mouse arrow in the middle of the picture and move the animal to the correct circle. Animals that both walk and swim would be in the middle part of the Venn diagram.

I Found a Letter

Open the I Found a Letter template and read the letter. Now select the Rubber Stamp tool. Look through the rubber stamp pictures and find pictures that fit into the sentence. Use your imagination. When you find the picture you want, click on it and then click on the part of the sentence where it belongs.

Put in the Words

Open the Put in the Words template and write in the correct words to finish the sentence. Down at the bottom of the page you will find words that you can use. Select the Typewriter tool or select Goodies and then Type Text. Click on the font that you want from the bottom of the screen and be sure to click where you want the word to begin before you write it in.

#2412 Kid Pix: Simple Projects   84   © Teacher Created Materials, Inc.

Templates

Kid Pix Projects Templates *(cont.)*

Draw a Picture

Open the Draw a Picture template. Read the description on the screen. Draw pictures to match descriptions of colors. Choose some rubber stamps or use the Wacky Pencil to illustrate each color description.

Color Bears Template

Open the Color Bears template. Here you get to make rows of wonderful colored bears. The directions tell you to make one row of green bears, one row of orange bears, and one row of purple bears. Select the Rubber Stamp tool and look for the bear rubber stamp. Stamp the first bear next to the green one on the screen. To make it larger, hold down the shift key as you stamp the bear. Now, to make it green, select the Paint Can tool and the color green from the color palette. Put the tip of the Paint Can onto the bear. Click your mouse, and the bear turns green. Now make the other bears in the correct color.

Show a Number Problem

Open the Show a Number Problem template. When you open the template, you see four rectangles and four addition math problems. Your job is to use pictures to show with pictures the math problems. Use the Rubber Stamp tool and choose your pictures. Be sure when you are showing a problem that all of the graphics are the same. You have to add like things to like things. To show subtraction, draw a circle using the Wacky Pencil around the objects that need to be taken away.

Small, Medium, Large

Open the Small, Medium, Large template. When you open the template, you will see the screen filled with all sizes of objects. You need to look carefully to find the small, medium and large one of each individual object. Look for the largest and write the letter L. Select the medium size and write the letter M on it. Select the smallest size and write the letter S on it. To write the letter, select the Typewriter tool and choose a font from the bottom of the page. If you want to make capital letters, hold down the shift key while you type in the letter.

Make a Jungle

When you open the screen, you see a jungle scene without any animals. Where have they gone? All you have on the screen are the names of the animals. You need to find them. Look in the Rubber Stamp options to find the animals and put them on the screen. Thank goodness, you found them all.

© *Teacher Created Materials, Inc.* 85 *##2412 Kid Pix: Simple Projects*

Templates

Kid Pix Projects Templates *(cont.)*

The Five Senses

Open the Five Senses template and notice the large circle with the five senses written on it, one in each section. Notice also that there is one picture for a sense each section. Your job is to use the Rubber Stamp tool and rubber stamp options to find more pictures to go in each section.

There should be at least five in each section. Some pictures can be used to show more than one sense.

Templates

Animal Venn Diagram

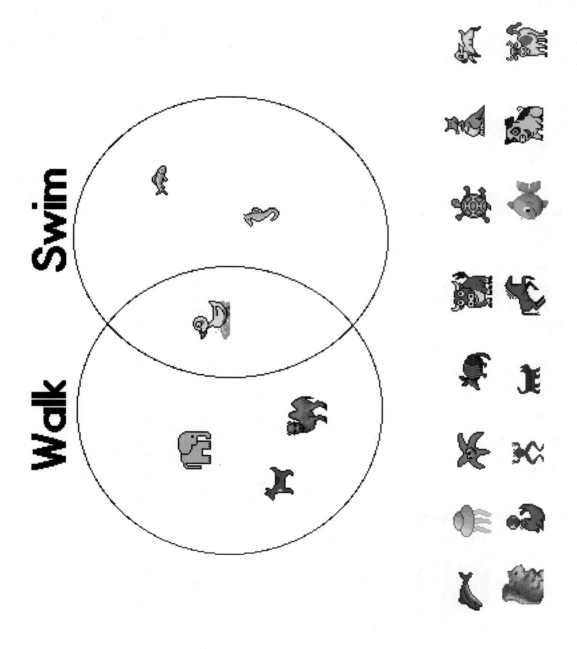

© Teacher Created Materials, Inc. 87 ##2412 Kid Pix: Simple Projects

Templates

I Found a Letter

I Found a Letter

I opened the   and I found an invitation to a   .

The   is for a   .

We are supposed to wear   .

Instead of presents, we are to bring   .

The party is going to be at the   .

We are going to eat   .

#2412 Kid Pix: Simple Projects   88   © Teacher Created Materials, Inc.

Templates

Put in the Words

Put in the words.

This is the way I wash my _____
This is the way I wash my _____
This is the way I wash my _____
So early in the morning.

hair   legs   face   feet   arms

© Teacher Created Materials, Inc.   89   ##2412 Kid Pix: Simple Projects

Draw a Picture

Draw a picture for each sentence.

Black is "boom, boom, boom!

White is a cherry bloom.

Black is a smokestack

White is a light foot walking.

Color Bears

Make one row of green bears.
Make one row of orange bears.
Make one row of purple bears.

Show a Number Problem

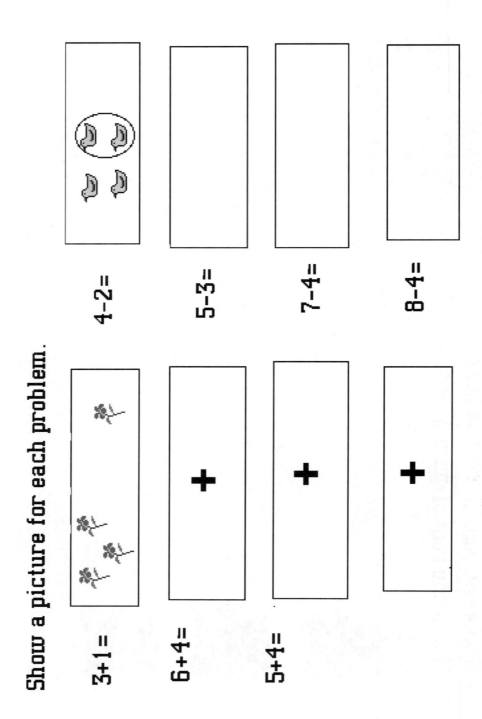

Templates

#2412 Kid Pix: Simple Projects

Templates

Small, Medium, Large

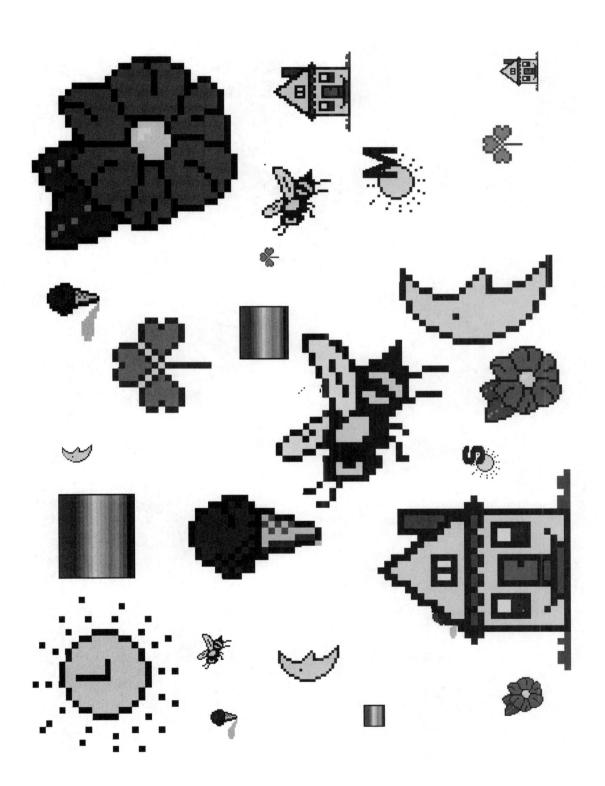

Make a Jungle

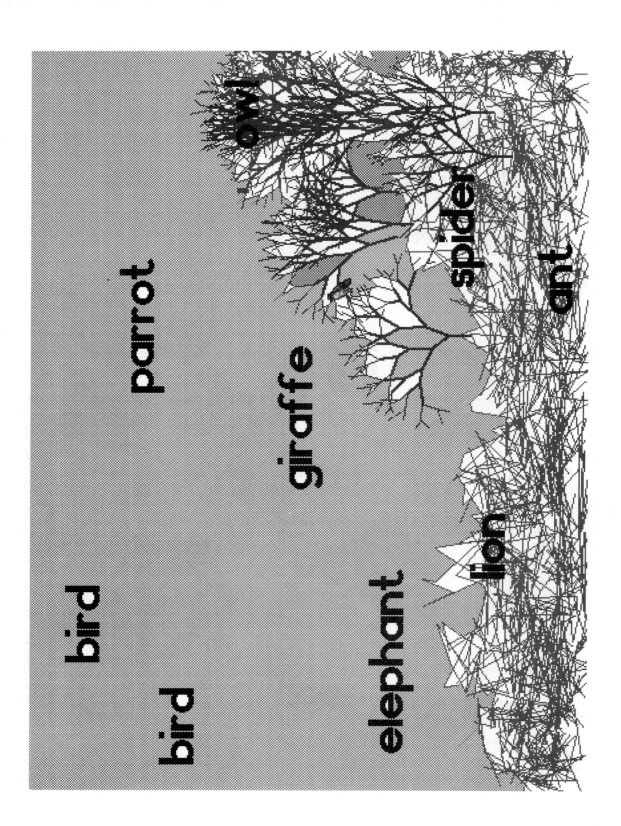

Templates

The Five Senses

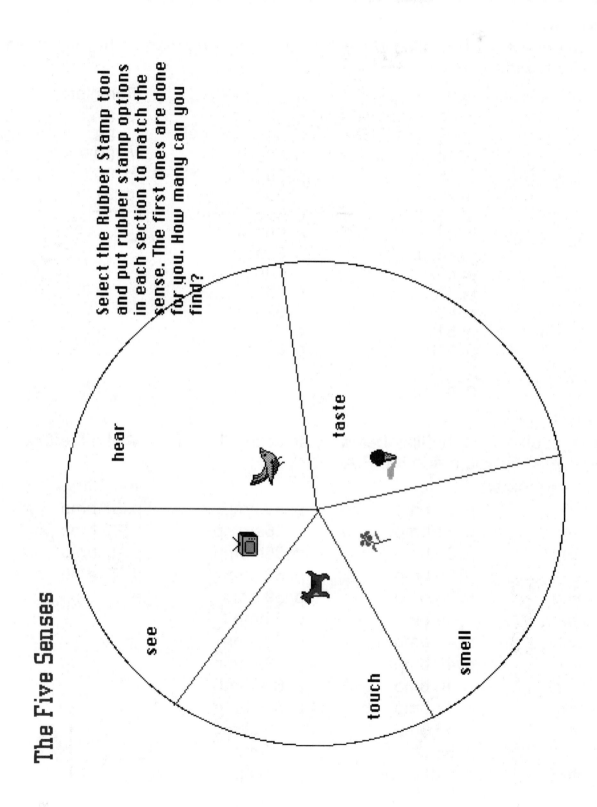

The Five Senses

Select the Rubber Stamp tool and put rubber stamp options in each section to match the sense. The first ones are done for you. How many can you find?

© Teacher Created Materials, Inc.   95   ##2412 Kid Pix: Simple Projects

Templates

The CD-ROM

Macintosh Files

You can open any of the files below by double-clicking them. They will open automatically in Kid Pix.

Samples (a folder)

			Templates (a folder)	
p. 10	p. 30	p. 53	p. 87	p. 92
p. 11	p. 31	p. 56a	p. 88	p. 93
p. 12	p. 34	p. 56b	p. 89	p. 94
p. 13	p. 35	p. 58	p. 90	p. 95
p. 14	p. 38	p. 59	p. 91	
p. 17a	p. 39	p. 6		
p. 17b	p. 42	p. 60		
p. 18a	p. 45. tiff	p. 63a		
p. 18b	p. 46	p. 63b		
p. 20	p. 47	p. 63c		
p. 21	p. 48	p. 63d		
p. 23	p. 51a	p. 7		
p. 24	p. 51b	p. 8		
p. 27	p. 51c			
p. 28	p. 52			

Windows Files

You can open any of the files below by selecting them from within the Open dialog box while you are in Kid Pix.

Samples (a folder)

			Templates (a folder)	
p. 10.bmp	p. 30.bmp	p. 53.bmp	p. 87.bmp	p. 92.bmp
p. 11.bmp	p. 31.bmp	p. 56a.bmp	p. 88.bmp	p. 93.bmp
p. 12.bmp	p. 34.bmp	p. 56b.bmp	p. 89.bmp	p. 94.bmp
p. 13.bmp	p. 35.bmp	p. 58.bmp	p. 90.bmp	p. 95.bmp
p. 14.bmp	p. 38.bmp	p. 59.bmp	p. 91.bmp	
p. 17a.bmp	p. 39.bmp	p. 6.bmp		
p. 17b.bmp	p. 42.bmp	p. 60.bmp		
p. 18a.bmp	p. 45.bmp	p. 63a.bmp		
p. 18b.bmp	p. 46.bmp	p. 63b.bmp		
p. 20.bmp	p. 47.bmp	p. 63c.bmp		
p. 21.bmp	p. 48.bmp	p. 63d.bmp		
p. 23.bmp	p. 51a.bmp	p. 7.bmp		
p. 24.bmp	p. 51b.bmp	p. 8.bmp		
p. 27.bmp	p. 51c.bmp			
p. 28.bmp	p. 52.bmp			